The Wife The Warrior

Help! Jezebel Has Seduced My Husband

Apostle Deborah Edwards

For information/contact: e-mail: dedwards@dreemm.org
DREEMM, P.O. Box 40292, Cincinnati, Ohio 45240.

Printed in the United States of America; Published, 2019.
Copyright © 2019 - Deborah Edwards.
ISBN# 978-0-9857400-8-5

Bride/Warrior sketch drawing design by artist Jeremiah Ford, used by permission.

THE WIFE THE WARRIOR
(HELP! JEZEBEL HAS SEDUCED MY HUSBAND)

TABLE OF CONTENTS

Dedication

I would like to first thank God for seeing me through some of the most challenging years of my life. Through the experiences contained in this book, I have come to realize the reality of Romans 8:28-29 (AMP).

"And we know [with great confidence] that God [who is deeply concerned about us] causes all things to work together [as a plan] for good for those who love God, to those who are called according to His plan and purpose. For those whom He foreknew [and loved and chose beforehand], He also predestined to be conformed to the image of His Son [and ultimately share in His complete sanctification], so that He would be the firstborn [the most beloved and honored] among many believers."

*I would like to dedicate this book to my husband,
Michael. Without your love and support this
work would not have been possible. Thank
you for being on this journey with me.
Thank you for praying for me
and fighting for us.*

*To my parents, Willie and Vera, you both have been
amazing parents and role models. You have always
encouraged me and demonstrated your love
in so many ways. I am the woman, wife
and mother that I am today, because
of what you taught and modeled
before me.*

*To my daughters, Tiffany, Talecia and Dana, I owe you
all so much gratitude. Your presence in my life gave
me strength to push forward, when I did not want
to. I now pass on to you and every reader of this
book the 'baton of victory'. When the enemy
comes after your marriage, just hold up
this book as a reminder to him, that
you now possess the strategies
to defeat him.*

I love you all.

Foreword

Apostle Deborah Edwards is a known regional expert in the area of Deliverance and brings that expertise to adaptation in her book, *The Wife The Warrior (Help! Jezebel Has Seduced My Husband)*. The book introduces Jezebel to the reader who may not be familiar with her and her intentionally destructive tactics, especially in the marriage union. Although Deborah Edwards is writing from the voice of a wife, anyone can benefit from her exposure of this wicked spirit; because the book includes information, tips, and strategies that will also help married men, and can serve as a powerful book to prepare couples in counseling while planning for marriage.

Apostle Deborah takes the reader on a chapter by chapter journey explaining: the stages of seduction, revealing extracts on conviction, showing what appears to be marital bliss, describing the supernatural awakening, depicting several specifics of the battle, and she eloquently ends the journey disclosing a heartfelt picture of victory over Jezebel's attacks!

The Wife The Warrior is unique in that Apostle Edwards has blended the expository style of writing with the narrative style synchronously captivating the reading audience with her personal life's story, while walking through her own experiences leading to triumph over forces against her marriage. Deborah's personal transparency moves the reader to want to learn and apply every strategy given in the book. Moreover, the author directs the reader to use prayer foci, points to remember, and prayer strategies at the end of each chapter. These activations prompt self-initiation of the success models given in each chapter. The glossary of terms is an added support to understanding who the warfare is against, and how to stand one's ground for imminent victory.

As a personal friend and colleaque in ministry, thank you Apostle Deborah Edwards for sharing even the bitter of your life to make my life a whole lot sweeter.

As a professional, I avouch that the content of Apostle Deborah's book is interwoven with solid Biblical scriptures that support her literary voice and view about a wife becoming both a bride and a warrior in order to fight for, and enjoy the blessedness and happiness God intended for marriage. Without reservation, this book, *The Wife The Warrior (Help! Jezebel Has Seduced My Husband),* is a "must read" for healing and saving those considering and those committed to the covenant of marriage!

Dr. Cecilia Jackson,
Apostle ("I AM" Fellowship Ministries, USA)

Preface

It is one thing when your husband's heart has been lured away from you by another woman, but what happens when the perpetrator is something you can't see, touch or feel? When you can't smell her perfume and when there's no lip stick on his collar and no unknown text or phone number, then what mode of action does the wife take?

There will come a time in most marriages, especially those that are ordained by God, that you as a wife will have to trade in your bouquet for a sword and fight for your marriage; fight for your family. This book serves as a guide as well as a testimony to you, that you can and will have victory.

> Ephesians 6:10-18 (AMPC) "In conclusion, be strong in the Lord [be empowered through your union with Him]; draw your strength from Him [that strength which His boundless might provides]. Put on God's whole armor [the armor of a heavy-armed soldier which God supplies], that you may be able successfully to stand up against [all] the strategies and the deceits of the devil. For we are not wrestling with flesh and blood [contending only with physical opponents], but against the despotisms, against the powers, against [the master spirits who are] the world rulers of this present darkness, against the spirit forces of wickedness in the heavenly (supernatural) sphere. Therefore put on God's complete armor, that you may be able to re-sist and stand your ground on the evil day [of danger], and, having done all [the crisis demands], to stand [firmly in your place]. Stand therefore [hold your ground], having tightened the belt of truth around your loins and having put on the

breastplate of integrity and of moral rectitude and right standing with God, And having shod your feet in preparation [to face the enemy with the firm-footed stability, the promptness, and the readiness produced by the good news] of the Gospel of peace. Lift up over all the [covering] shield of saving faith, upon which you can quench all the flaming missiles of the wicked [one]. And take the helmet of salvation and the sword that the Spirit wields, which is the Word of God. Pray at all times (on every occasion, in every season) in the Spirit, with all [manner of] prayer and entreaty. To that end keep alert and watch with strong purpose and perseverance, interceding on behalf of all the saints (God's consecrated people)."

Introduction

As a Deliverance teacher, trainer, and participant, I must admit that all of the teaching, the training, the tears, the missteps, the prayers and the hits and misses, truly prepared me for the journey I am about to take you on.

Over the past 38 years, all of the positions I've held included being an on-the-job-instructor (OJI); now, by the power of His might, and the victory through His blood, I can say that I am an OJI in the spirit against this unwelcomed intruder, Jezebel. To truly uncover and dismantle Jezebel and her army and to truly stop their attempts to destroy my marriage, the mechanics were not enough (i.e. classes, study manuals, conferences). Oh yes, there were books about Jezebel and there were books about being a wife, but never one that informed me that my spouse could be seduced by a spirit; especially one that I allowed to come in.

My hope and prayer are that as you read the pages of this book, you will be able to recognize the enemy in your situation and utilize the tools and strategies I had to learn in battle, so that your figh will not be extended and tedious.

> Titus 2:2-5 (MSG) "Your job is to speak out on the things that make for solid doctrine. Guide older men into lives of temperance, dignity, and wisdom, into healthy faith, love, and endurance. Guide older women into lives of reverence so they end up as neither gossips nor drunks, but models of goodness. By looking at them, the younger women will know how to love their

husbands and children, be virtuous and pure, keep a good house, be good wives. We don't want anyone looking down on God's Message because of their behavior."

Why should you read this book? There are many reasons; but the main one is that Our Heavenly Father wants His daughters free and happy. Sometimes we have to fight for that freedom!

Not only did Jesus come into the earth for our salvation but it was also to provide the opportunity for us to have abundant life. In the following scripture text, He not only lets us know what HIs purpose Is; simultaneously, He reveals the plans of the enemy.

> John 10:9-11 (ASV) "I am the door; by me if any man enter in, he shall be saved, and shall go in and go out, and shall find pasture. The thief cometh not, but that he may steal, and kill, and destroy: I came that they may have life, and may have it abundantly. I am the good shepherd: the good shepherd layeth down his life for the sheep."

The abundant life message and promises were such a threat to the kingdom of darkness, that the enemy of our soul launched an unsuccessful attempt to prevent the message from getting to us. First, there was the murder of all newborn males.

> Matthew 2:1-18 (ASV) "Now when Jesus was born in Bethlehem of Judaea in the days of Herod the king, behold, Wise-men from the east came to Jerusalem, saying, Where is he that is born King of the Jews? for we saw his star in the east, and are come to worship him. And when Herod the king heard it, he was troubled, and all Jerusalem with him. Now when they were

departed, behold, an angel of the Lord appeareth to Joseph in a dream, saying, Arise and take the young child and his mother, and flee into Egypt, and be thou there until I tell thee: for Herod will seek the young child to destroy him. And he arose and took the young child and his mother by night, and departed into Egypt; and was there until the death of Herod: that it might be fulfilled which was spoken by the Lord through the prophet, saying, Out of Egypt did I call my son. Then Herod, when he saw that he was mocked of the Wise-men, was exceeding wroth, and sent forth, and slew all the male children that were in Bethlehem, and in all the borders thereof, from two years old and under, according to the time which he had exactly learned of the Wise-men. Then was fulfilled that which was spoken through Jeremiah the prophet, saying, A voice was heard in Ramah, Weeping and great mourning, Rachel weeping for her children; And she would not be comforted, because they are not."

The last attempt was a premature death attempt. Notice in John 10:11, Jesus stated that the good shepherd lays down his life for His sheep. I am of the opinion that satan's plan was to have a fight ensue at the Garden of Gethsemane, but he temporarily had a moment of amnesia, forgot that Jesus really was the Son of God, and that He knows all things.

Ever wonder why he told the disciples to watch and pray? The role of the watchmen was to stand guard and watch for the enemy or impending danger.

> Mark 14:37-39 (ASV) "And he cometh, and findeth them sleeping, and saith unto Peter, Simon, sleepest thou? couldest thou not watch one hour? Watch and pray, that ye enter not into temptation: the spirit indeed is willing, but the flesh is weak. And again he went away, and prayed, saying the same words."

In the next two scripture texts, we see clearly that Jesus was trying to avoid all altercations:

1) So that prophesy could be fulfilled as it related to all of the disciples living through that particular night.

2) The second scripture reference, lets us know that Jesus knew the real intents of the hearts of those who came to capture him.

> Mark 14:45-49 (AMP) "When Judas came, immediately he went up to Jesus and said, "Rabbi (Master)!" and he kissed Him [forcefully]. They laid hands on Him and seized Him. But one of the bystanders [Simon Peter] drew his sword and struck [Malchus] the slave of the high priest and cut off his ear. Jesus said to them, "Have you come out with swords and clubs to arrest Me, as you would against a robber? Day after

You too may be going through a rough period in your marriage, but just as the disciples had their destiny to fulfill, so do you. You will make it through your hour of temptation; you will make it through your night time.

day I was with you, teaching in the [courts and porches of the] temple, and you did not seize Me; but this has happened so that the Scriptures would be fulfilled."

John 18:3-9 (TLB) "The chief priests and Pharisees had given Judas a squad of soldiers and police to accompany him. Now with blazing torches, lanterns, and weapons they arrived at the olive grove. Jesus fully realized all that was going to happen to him. Stepping forward to meet them he asked, "Whom are you looking for?" "Jesus of Nazareth," they replied. "I am he," Jesus said. And as he said it, they all fell backwards to the ground! Once more he asked them, "Whom are you searching for?" And again they replied, "Jesus of Nazareth." "I told you I am he," Jesus said; "and since I am the one you are after, let these others go." He did this to carry out the prophecy he had just made, "I have not lost a single one of those you gave me . . ."

So, you see, from the announcement of Christ's birth to the finished work of the cross, the enemy has tried to stop your abundant life; your fruitful marriage; your joy unspeakable; and of course, your peace that surpasses all understanding. As Jesus was committed to not losing one of those that was given to Him, He is not willing to lose you nor the representation of His covenant in the earth, which is your marriage.

> Philippians 4:6-7 (AMP) "Do not be anxious or worried about anything, but in everything [every circumstance and situation] by prayer and petition with thanksgiving, continue to make your [specific] requests known to God. And the peace of God [that peace which reassures the heart, that peace] which transcends all understanding, [that peace which] stands guard over your hearts and your minds in Christ Jesus [is yours]."

The contents of *The Wife The Warrior* will help you to identify the enemy, recognize your weapons, recognize the weapons that the enemy will attempt to use against you, and equip you to fight him, overtake him and dismantle any and all strongholds he has built against you. You will learn of generational curses and cycles, familiar spirits and their role, obedience vs. disobedience, and how to prepare for war!

You will learn and understand how demonic groupings work and how they join together to strengthen their stance against you and fortify their efforts to destroy your marriage. You will be able to recognize the spirit spouse (incubus/succubus), whispering spirits, the accuser of the brethren, strife, bitterness, anger, the spirit of python, perversion and many more spirits when they come to take their turn to try to destroy you and your family. The enemy is not satisfied with you being unhappy in your marriage, or even separated. He wants your marriage vows abolished and the marriage contract destroyed as a testament against our Lord and God. Stand your ground, put on your armor and let's prepare for war!

PRAYER FOCUS - Lord, let me not become weary while trying to do well. Help me to make good decisions and choices. Help me to have the faith and confidence in You that I need, that assures me that I will reap of your goodness and the abundant life if I don't give up.

REMEMBER:
- Your marriage is a representation of God's covenant in the earth.
- God has a plan for your life and He will not abandon you.

PRAYER STRATEGY - Purchase a prayer journal and notebook strictly for your marriage. Begin to build your personal arsenal with scriptures based on the promises of God for your marriage. Write down what the Holy Spirit tells you to write and follow His lead.

Chapter 1

Who is Jezebel?

I am writing this book from a wife's perspective because the events are from portions of my life's story. Typically, we view Jezebel as a tempter of men; however, a woman can be seduced by Jezebel also, as you will soon learn.

I am applying the "law of first mention", in order to gain a better concept of the subject matter, Jezebel. The first time that we hear of Jezebel is in 1 Kings 16:30-32. These three verses of scripture are packed with information about her. Knowing who her father was and the god he served, provides a lot of insight into who Jezebel was and why the spirit of Jezebel would be so strongly against marriages and families.

> 1 Kings 16:30-32 (KJV) "And Ahab the son of Omri did evil in the sight of the LORD above all that were before him. And it came to pass, as if it had been a light thing for him to walk in the sins of Jeroboam the son of Nebat, that he took to wife Jezebel the daughter of Ethbaal king of the Zidonians, and went and served Baal, and worshipped him. And he reared up an altar for Baal in the house of Baal, which he had built in Samaria."

This text shows that Jezebel's history reflects a generational pattern of yoking up (connecting) through marriages and family so that an entire belief system can be compromised. Such compromise and destruction of marriages and families eventually leads to the destruction of entire nations. This arrangement was definitely not love at first sight, but more like the seasonal show, "Married at First Sight".

Jezebel's arising was a political move. Her father was not only king but functioned as a high priest also. Jezebel being Ahab's daughter grew up as the custom dictated, serving an array of gods; Baal was the chief. They were also descedants of the Canaanites, so to get an even clearer picture of the function of this spirit, let's review both Baal and the Canaanites' history.

> Genesis 9:21-26 (KJV) "And he drank of the wine, and was drunken; and he was uncovered within his tent. And Ham, the father of Canaan, saw the nakedness of his father, and told his two brethren without. And Shem and Japheth took a garment, and laid it upon both their shoulders, and went backward, and covered the nakedness of their father; and their faces were backward, and they saw not their father's nakedness. And Noah awoke from his wine, and knew what his younger son had done unto him. And he said, Cursed be Canaan; a servant of servants shall he be unto his brethren."

From the beginning we see there is a lack of honor for righteousness and no respect for family. Some people think Jezebel introduced Baal when she married Ahab, but the following scriptures let us know that some of the Israelites were secretly worshipping Baal even after they had been warned by God not to do so.

> Deuteronomy 6:14-15 (KJV) "Ye shall not go after other gods, of the gods of the people which are round about you; (For the LORD thy God is a jealous God among you) lest the anger of the LORD thy God be kindled against thee, and destroy thee from off the face of the earth."

Judges 3:5-7 (KJV) "And the children of Israel dwelt among the Canaanites, Hittites, and Amorites, and Perizzites, and Hivites, and Jebusites: And they took their daughters to be their wives, and gave their daughters to their sons, and served their gods. And the children of Israel did evil in the sight of the LORD, and forgot the LORD their God, and served Baalim and the groves."

When Jezebel arrived Ahab so wanted to please her; therefore once she became his queen, King Ahab made it law that no one had to go into the mountains nor into hiding to worship Baal. This ungodly decision prompted God to say that Ahab had sinned worse than all those that were before him. Baal was also known as the god of fertility, he wanted to produce after himself. Hence, it was Jezebel's objective to turn an entire nation over to Baal causing them to worship him and him only. If she was able to bully, intimidate and manipulate an entire nation, what limits would she go to in order to destroy a marriage that was destined to give God glory; especially a marriage that's not aware of her invasion nor her strategies? Remember, anyone who would not convert to Baal Jezebel destroyed. "The thief cometh not but to steal, kill and destroy," John 10:10 (KJV).

When dealing with the spirit of Jezebel, we have to remember that spirits never work alone. Demons always travel in groups.

The demonic grouping for a Jezebelic Network could include, but is not limited to:

- the spirit of rejection (past hurts and wounds)
- the spirit of deception
- a lying spirit

- the spirit of manipulation
- the spirit of control
- the spirit of pride
- blinding and blocking spirits

The following are characteristics of this spirit and examples of how they might manifest in the attack against your marriage:

Jezebel is **clairvoyant**
Jezebel **deceives**
Jezebel **destroys**
Jezebel **discredits**
Jezebel **divides**
Jezebel is **domineering**
Jezebel **intimidates**
Jezebel **lies**
Jezebel **manipulates**
Jezebel **murders**
Jezebel is **relentless**
Jezebel is **revengeful**
Jezebel **seduces**
Jezebel **sows seeds of discord**
Jezebel **steals**

Now that you know some of the character traits and manifestations of Jezebel, what are some of the natural warning signs of infidelity whom this spirit targets for marriages?

Your spouse will begin to withdraw physically and emotionally. You will notice that what you use to do as a family, your spouse will no longer want to be involved with. Unfortunately, and initially, this change may not manifest in your sex life, but if not stopped, it soon will. In this scenario there are a trio of demonic spirits manifesting, the main one being rejection.

Your spouse will begin to isolate from you and the family. He or she may stay on the computer every waking hour, be glued to the phone or any other electronic gadget, or become immersed with any activity that can be done alone. He or she will have little to no desire to socialize with friends or family and may even try to get you to separate from your support system. This is an example of a caging spirit invading the scene. Its responsibility is to build a fortress or cage to house all of the spirits that are present in your spouse's soul, and those that are on the way.

Your spouse will begin the blame game or fault-finding strategy. Everything that goes wrong is said to be your fault. If sexual engagement happens too fast in the bedroom, it's your fault. If he was late for work, it's your fault. If there aren't any groceries in the house, it's your fault. If he gets lost driving, it's your fault. This spirit is known as "The Victim". This spirit normally enters in through a childhood incident or traumatic experience that occurs at a young age, but lies dormant until the appropriate time or until it gains strengthen from uniting with other spirits.

Identity crisis. Your spouse may be aware that something is going on but believes it surely cannot be with him. At this stage of the attack, blinding and blocking spirits have been added to what will soon become a fortress building a stronghold in your spouse's soul. The blinding and blocking spirits function to keep your spouse from recognizing his need for help, deliverance or repentance. His/her very identity is beginning to change and being pulled toward darkness.

The **blinding spirit** is there to prevent your spouse from seeing truth and identifying him (the demon). Whereas the blocking spirit is there to prevent him from hearing truth and from hearing you. You may say one thing but your spouse will hear something totally different. When this begins to happen, a spirit that we will call *"wicker"* is now a part of the team. Wicker's role is to twist the truth. Although not called "wicker" but rather called the "serpent" in Genesis in the Garden of Eden, the function is the same. It takes truth and twists it in order to deceive you.

The longer these spirits go unchallenged the more it will appear to your spouse that you are the enemy. The enemy through your spouse is setting your marriage up for the fall - your fall. The Jezebel spirit while operating through one spouse will always try to make the other spouse look like the manipulating, controlling, self-centered, never satisfied spouse.

Character Assassination. I remember being in marriage ministry one night, and I begin to share the story of how my husband had swept me off of my feet (I'll provide more details later). Every time I would share a memory, he would say, *"I don't remember that"*. After he made this statement several times, one of the brothers became so irritated with him that he yelled at him and said, "Man she is paying you a compliment". My husband was quiet and I was hurt. Face it ladies, no matter how disrespectful a husband may be to us, behind closed doors, there is still a part of us that desires to help our mate and cover them. We were created to help them, but there will come a time when exposure will come and it will be necessary. Demons try to hide and as long as you as a spouse are the only witness, demons are satisfied, but the minute their presence becomes known to others they will enlist the help of other demonic spirits to strengthen their stronghold, their fortress around you.

> Genesis 2:18 (NKJV) "And the LORD God said, "It is not good that man should be alone; I will make him a helper comparable to him."

I had been sharing our testimony for over 20 years, and was consistent with the events, which always detailed our brief whirlwind courtship, yet, if my husband was present, he would say, *"I don't remember that".* One day, I asked him why did he want people to think that I was a liar? *I did not know that Jezebel was present and plotting.* I did not have a clear understanding of all that God was calling us into, but the enemy knew more than I did and was already trying to *destroy my character, destroy my reputation, and destroy my marriage.* God called the two of us. His plan did not just include me, but my husband also. *The Jezebelic Network will try to destroy how your husband sees you, so it can cause your husband to influence how others see you.*

When the attack becomes so fierce that you feel as if you can hardly make it, take confidence and find strength in knowing that *the enemy is more afraid of you and your purpose then you are of him and his assignment.* He must try to instill fear, doubt, and hopelessness within you so that your vision will become cloudy, your hearing dull, and your heart overwhelmed. He must change how your spouse sees you, causing loss of respect for you and an identity crisis in the marriage, so that the spouse no longer sees you as part of him/her. You have the key! Wives you were created to be a helper for and to your husband. The enemy must change the idea of your role, so that division can enter in, making the two, *INDIVIDUALS AND NOT ONE FLESH.*

Psalm 61:1-3 (AMP) "Hear my cry, O God; Listen to my prayer. From the end of the earth I call to You, when my heart is overwhelmed and weak; Lead me to the rock that is higher than I [a rock that is too high to reach without Your help]. For You have been a shelter and a refuge for me, A strong tower against the enemy."

Rejection. This attack and process to divide the two of you could cause both of you to feel rejected by the other. Let's face it, we all have been attacked by this spirit at one time or another. What we need to focus on is the event or action that caused us to feel rejected, because that is where the inner healing and deliverance will begin. The hurt or wound of rejection is there long before the actual spirit working thru rejection enters on the scene and attaches itself to the wound, scar, or emotions. Whatever happened to us is what produced a wound, which did not get addressed or healed. When that wound stays there unattended and unaddressed, soon a demon will notice and move in to set up house.

God is a relational God and He created us to be relational. Imagine your spouse, your friend, or even yourself, with chains and locks covering your body and binding you. You may have one of the keys that fits one of the locks on your husband or friend and they may have a key that will free you. The problem is that the enemy is aware of the keys that we carry for each other, especially those that we carry for our spouse. Therefore, *one of the tactics of the enemy is to cause strife, division, and dissention between the two of you, so that you can never get close enough to place your key in the lock that controls the chains that are binding. For those of you who have a prophetic eye, strife will appear in your bed as a snake.* I have made it a practice to sit back, pray, and observe, whenever I am in a new relationship with someone and we clash like nobody's business. I then ask God; do I have a key for them or do they have one for me?

> Matthew 16:19 (AMP) "I will give you the keys (authority) of the kingdom of heaven; and whatever you bind [forbid, declare to be improper and unlawful] on earth will have [already] been bound in heaven, and whatever you loose [permit, declare lawful] on earth will have [already] been loosed in heaven."

The Man. When a man's soul is injured as a little boy, his emotional and psychological development is delayed. His body continues to grow, his looks continue to change, but emotionally he is a dwarf. Inner healing is necessary; it is vitally important to the health of his marriage and the well-being of his children.

When these previously mentioned spirits are not recognized and therefore not challenged, not only do they set up house in the man's soul but they will now have access to his blood line. As his girlfriend, fiancée, and eventually his wife, you may not recognize these natural warning signs right away because he really doesn't want to be alone; therefore, he is going to put his "best foot forward."

Men were taught to *"man-up"*; *"don't wimp out"*; and of course, the biggest lie of them all, *"men don't cry"*. In actuality it takes a real man to be able to be in touch with his feelings, his emotions and say, *"Help! I need help"*. What a joy it is when a married man contending with demonic traffic realizes that his wife really is his help-meet; his collaborator and partner; someone especially designed to help meet his needs ... suitable just for him. The realization that his wife is not his adversary can shift the marriage from failure to the beginnings of deliverance.

Genesis 2:20-25 (KJV) "And Adam gave names to all cattle, and to the fowl of the air, and to every beast of the field; but for Adam there was not found an help meet for him. And the LORD God caused a deep sleep to fall upon Adam, and he slept: and he took one of his ribs, and closed up the flesh instead thereof; And the rib, which the LORD God had taken from man, made he a woman, and brought her unto the man. And Adam said, This is now bone of my bones, and flesh of my flesh: she shall be called Woman, because she was taken out of Man. Therefore shall a man leave his father and his mother, and shall cleave unto his wife: and they shall be one flesh. And they were both naked, the man and his wife, and were not ashamed."

The Woman. "Looking for love in all the wrong places", that's what rejection looks like in and on the female. Her emotional growth is also stunted. For some women, their looks can be deceiving. Some may appear to have everything together, while others may take on the look and attitude of rejection (weariness, depression and sadness), desiring to be rescued, but doing everything to sabotage the rescue efforts because they believe they are supposed to feel that way. At this stage, women are not only experiencing rejection, but now "perceived" rejection and "self-rejection" have taken a seat in the soul. There is a void, and only Jesus can fill that void. The wound of rejection has to be healed first.

With all three in place (rejection, perceived and self-rejection), the person's vision is not balanced (or out of alignment), their thinking is out of alignment. What may be rational to everyone else, is irrational to them. Their thinking becomes twisted and when correction comes, they dismiss it because it is viewed as someone trying to control them or someone doesn't want them to be happy. They feel rejected.

This spirit of rejection now becomes one of the strongest opposing factors in the marriage. The actions of both will cause the other to feel rejected, unwanted, undesirable, and disrespected. At this point, someone should pursue the presence of God. All it takes to dismantle this nest are a few simple steps.

> James 4:6-8 (ASV) "But he giveth more grace. Wherefore the scripture saith, God resisteth the proud, but giveth grace to the humble. Be subject therefore unto God; but resist the devil, and he will flee from you. Draw nigh to God, and he will draw nigh to you. Cleanse your hands, ye sinners; and purify your hearts, ye double minded."

The spirit of rejection never operates alone and because there are at least three forms of rejection, one of them will be connected to some incident or memory, although, neither the incident nor the memory has to be true. Rejection can either be imposed, inflicted by others, inherent, or generational. Most are derived from a wounded spirit or soul. You will also notice a spirit of abandonment, the accuser of the brethren, a spirit of jealousy and envy, a whispering spirit, and hatred, accompanying the spirit of rejection. We will discuss these later.

> James 1:19-20 (AMP) "Understand this, my beloved brothers and sisters. Let everyone be quick to hear [be a careful, thoughtful listener], slow to speak [a speaker of carefully chosen words and], slow to anger [patient, reflective, forgiving]; for the [resentful, deep-seated] anger of man does not produce the righteousness of God [that standard of behavior which He requires from us]."

Remember, just as the enemy has been assigned to your spouse, there are some that have been assigned to you also. Their hope is that you would become so focused on your spouse that you won't notice them creeping into your mind and soul.

> Philippians 4:6-8 (AMP) "Do not be anxious or worried about anything, but in everything [every circumstance and situation] by prayer and petition with thanksgiving, continue to make your [specific] requests known to God. And the peace of God [that peace which reassures the heart, that peace] which transcends all understanding, [that peace which] stands guard over your hearts and your minds in Christ Jesus [is yours]. Finally, believers, whatever is true, whatever is honorable and worthy of respect, whatever is right and confirmed by God's word, whatever is pure and wholesome, whatever is lovely and brings peace, whatever is admirable and of good repute; if there is any excellence, if there is anything worthy of praise, think continually on these things [center your mind on them, and implant them in your heart]."

PRAYER FOCUS - Lord, please give me eyes to see and ears to hear. Guard my soul and heart against offense. When I become weak, please send me help. Give me wisdom and insight to the devices of the enemy. Help me to remember that my spouse is not my enemy.

REMEMBER:
- Rejection never works alone.
- Inner healing (the healing of your soul) is a necessity.
- Know whose you are and who you are: say "no" to identity theft.
- There is power and strength in unity: ask for help.
- Your marriage is a representation of Christ's Covenant in the earth.

PRAYER STRATEGY: Exodus 17:12 (AMP) "But Moses' hands were heavy and he grew tired. So they took a stone and put it under him, and he sat on it. Then Aaron and Hur held up his hands, one on one side and one on the other side; so it was that his hands were steady until the sun set."

During this season of understanding who Jezebel is, you too may need an Aaron and Hur, to lift your hands, so that you can worship through the pain; worship through the rejection; and worship through the confusion, until the sun sets (the attack is over, it is finished). Pray and ask the Father to send you someone especially designed and commissioned to help you.

In the book by Hannah Harnard, *"Hinds Feet in High Places"*, the main character "Much Afraid", had to go on a journey that was filled with many difficulties and challenges. The Good Shepherd, knew the terrain of the journey, and He also knew the outcome and what the journey would produce and develop within Much Afraid. Therefore, the Good Shepherd sent her two companions to journey with her. As she traveled on this journey, not only was Much Afraid changed and healed but so were the ones who stood by her side.

God has a plan and He knows just how to carry it out and just who to send to walk with you, strengthen you, and protect you during this journey. Ask Him!

This chapter was strategically designed to help you with the questions, Who Is Jezebel, and How does she operate within the marriage or pre-marriage relationship? Once completing the chapter, progress to the next chapter, "The Seduction." It is advisable to re-read and study Chapter One, if necessary, before moving into the next chapter. This text is intended to impel you in your personal journey on how to be *The Wife, The Warrior.*

Chapter 2

The Seduction: Open Doors

In the previous chapter we discussed some of the character traits and manifestations of Jezebel, some of the natural warning signs of infidelity, and the role of rejection as a partner with the Jezebelic Network to destroy your marriage. Unfortunately, most of us do not realize that we are seeing through the lenses of rejection. All we know is that we made it through the last relationship and we are moving forward. Moving forward with wounds and without Christ as your Personal Savior can be devastating.

I was raised in church my entire life. My first memory of feeling embarrassed as it relates to my Christian experience had to be around the age 5. It was Easter morning. My dress was pretty and my hat and gloves matched my socks with the lace around them. I was feeling very pretty until my cousin noticed that my legs were ashy. With all of that shopping and getting the hair pressed and curled, somebody forgot to buy lotion, so my mother took biscuits from the morning breakfast and rubbed them between her hands to get the shortening and butter out of them and rubbed them on our legs. I went to church all dressed up and smelling like a biscuit. Memories like that began to shape an incorrect self-identity. I did not realize it then, nor was I able to comprehend what was happening to my view of myself. I realize now, that incident was the beginning of my altered sense of identity. I was no longer able to think of myself as the pretty little girl with the pretty dress, but rather the girl that smelled like a biscuit. Therefore, the identity of "less than", and "not good enough" and "just plain different or beneath others", began to form.

I continued to go to church and even started singing in the choir, attending Sunday School and all the activities for the children, the youth, and then the teenagers. I sang at church; I competed in music competitions at school. I learned to play the violin, the viola and the cello. By the time I was in my late teens, I had been in church on Saturdays, all day on Sundays and during midweek service, *(when we had transportation)*; but with all of that time in "church", I didn't know Jesus. I don't remember being taught that I needed Him as my personal Savior. Savior, what's that? You mean to tell me that some of those Easter speeches were more than words to say on Easter morning?

I was one of the lead singers in our youth choir. At the time, I was dating the Bishop's and Pastor's grandson. I was singing a song that had a musical run where I would just say, "Jesus, Jesus, Jesus, Jesus (3x), Oh Jesus, He is my everything". The Pastor stood up with tears in her eyes and yelled, "Call on Him child, 'cause you're gonna' need Him!" I began to cry too.

Why was I going to need Him? What did she know? What insight did she have into my destiny that made her fear for me? Then, I was scared. To combat my own fears, I convinced myself that she only said that because she knew that her grandson was no good. Instead of my fears pushing me into God's Presence, (a Presence that I was not even aware of at the time) they took me further away from Him.

> *The enemy doesn't fight fair, he goes after our identity before we even realize that we have one.*

Not too long after that, a "prophet" came to town. He had me to stand up and begin to speak into my life. A prophet, are you kidding me? "Who/what, are they for real? Aren't they just in the Bible?" As he started to state what was going to happen to me, initially I thought, this is cute, until something hit me. The next thing I knew, I was in the pulpit sitting in the Bishop's chair, shaking like a pecan tree in the fall of Atlanta with "the hawk" at its best. I won't go into details here about everything; but, the key thing is that I was going to be moving a few states away and that I was going to be like the pastor, whom we referred to as "Ma Dear". Ma Dear, saw ghosts (demons) and I wanted no part of that. So I ran.

By the time I was 20, I was separated (from the pastor's grandson, my husband), with two beautiful girls that I was raising on my own. Afterwards I was dating a young man who was also dating a few other women. I would later find out about these other women when he was in a car accident. All these women started showing up at the hospital. First, my husband was unfaithful. Someone forgot to tell him that once you get married, you have to let your girlfriends go. Then, while dating the boyfriend, I found out I was not the only girl. I was at my limits.

Finally, I went searching for the God that had all of these promises for my life. I wanted to know if He was real or not. So I moved from Atlanta to Ohio. Sometime during the transition, what I know now as the Holy Spirit, began to teach me about the concept of marriage and the woman being taken from the rib of Adam. He wanted me to know that there was a man, a husband, just for me, and a father for my girls.

It would be years before I would meet him, and when I did, I didn't recognize him. You see, I still had on the lenses of "rejection"; the lenses of "perceived rejection"; and the lenses of "you're not good enough". I had met a few other imposters before my God-given husband came around and I was really fed up with men.

The guy I dated, prior to my husband, was a manager for a large petroleum company. He lived in a neighborhood that I could only have dreamt of living in at the time. He promised me the house, the car, and the world to see with him; but there was a catch. He wanted me to sleep with him first. He purchased expensive gifts for me, but wouldn't let me take possession of them unless I slept with him. He still has the gifts; I guess. I might not have been sure of who I was, but what was clear is that I knew I wasn't for sale.

The Jackson Five (singing group) was back together for a reunion tour. This gentleman had front row seats, and backstage passes at the hotel where the Jacksons were going to be staying. I was so excited; I was an adult but I still had a school girl's crush on Marlon Jackson! As excited as I was, something kept tugging on my insides, concerning sleeping arrangements. I addressed the issue with him and since I did not want to sleep in the same room with him, the trip was cancelled. At least I didn't go; he found someone else that went with him. I told him the next man that I slept with would be my husband. He said I was living in a dream world, and that I needed to remember that I had two children.

Again, rejected! Again not good enough and what's worst, we can now add bitterness to the mix. I wasn't insecure as it related to my appearance or my body shape. The men who were in my life proved to me that none of that mattered; one woman was just not enough and if she had children she was damaged in some way. Rejected, angry, and bitter; what a combination and I was still "in church".

Two weeks later I met my husband Michael. I had been so very mean and hateful to him when I was introduced to him and learned of his name. I was so rude that I became ashamed of myself and agreed to meet him face to face. I met him on a Sunday; he paid my gas bill that Thursday. A week after, he took my girls shopping for shoes. A week after that I promised him dinner for being so kind to me, and dinner was all he was going to get. I remember thinking, "Why is he being so nice to me?"

Nope, nana, not a chance! I was NOT going to sleep with him. I did not ask him to do those things for me and I was not giving him anything but a meal, a thank you, and a "have a nice life".

To my surprise, he shocked me with a gesture that shook me, one that caused some of the walls I had built up through anger and rejection to start crumbling, and one gesture that I will always hold dear. *He said he needed to take me to the grocery store to purchase the food I would serve him for dinner, because he would never place his feet under my table if he didn't put the food on top of it.*

The next week Michael took me shopping to purchase everything that my girls wanted for Christmas. Initially, as he started to do these things for me, I got angry because I thought he was just like all of the other men who just wanted to sleep with me. As I would tell God that

---

> *I'll never place my feet under your table if I don't put the food on top of it.*

I didn't want him, the Lord would remind me of a letter that I wrote to Him detailing what I wanted in a husband.

After the Christmas shopping trip I begin to relax, relax too much. Michael never tried to come at me sexually, so I began to think that something was wrong with him or me.

After all, life had taught me several lessons: First, that I was undesirable to a man but if I gave him what he wanted (physical gratification) then maybe, just maybe, I would be desirable. Second, a man couldn't be trusted. Third, one woman was not enough for any man.

I did not know the love of a real man, nor did I know how I was supposed to be treated. When I asked Michael why he wasn't trying to sleep with me, he said, "because I know that you are a Christian, you may enjoy yourself tonight but you will hate yourself in the morning".

After being with this man for 5 weeks, he had already said that he loved me enough that he could spend the rest of his life with me without touching me. Now, I'm confused. Rather than taking him at his word, I'd rather believe this was another way to reject me.

This was a lie, right? Was it possible for a man to love a woman enough to keep her holy? Was it possible that there was a man who could control his own sexual desires because he felt like a woman was worth the wait? NOPE!!! Not in my world, but in God's Kingdom it is possible. The problem was that I had not heard of this teaching, nor the value of a virtuous woman, nor the words, "You are worthy of respect and honor."

Rejection blinded me from truth and my response would start me on a trajectory that was not part of God's will for my life. My response was, "Let me worry about the morning time."

I compromised my faith. I dishonored the God, who had not only transplanted me, but who had truly taken good care of me. Those words, with doubt and unbelief, lust, bitterness, and a wounded soul were all that Jezebel needed. It was a welcome mat for her to come into a marriage that had not even begun. So Jezebel showed up in me. That's right, it was there, it had found a place in my soul and was waiting on the right time to manifest. So imprudent, right? I opened the door. I sent the invitation. I did not count the cost.

I became friends with pride, as I had boldly taken a stand of righteousness with the last guy. With everything that he had dangled in front of me, I would not give in. Now this man was not dangling anything, he was giving to me from his heart and I did not know how to handle it. Pride comes before a fall and fall I did; almost to the point of not being able or desiring to get up. I just wanted to die.

> Proverbs 16:17-18 (MSG) "The road of right living bypasses evil; watch your step and save your life. First pride, then the crash — the bigger the ego, the harder the fall."

PRAYER FOCUS - Father, heal me from my brokenness. Place Your healing balm on the wounds and gashes in my heart. Forgive me, for I have sinned against You and man.

REMEMBER TO:
- Stay focused.
- Do not compromise.
- You are more than enough.
- Your actions and reactions do not just affect you.
- Don't send Jezebel and invitation, she will gladly accept it.
- Count the cost.
- You are worth honor and respect.

PRAYER STRATEGY - Psalms 51:11-13 (KJV) "Cast me not away from thy presence; and take not thy holy spirit from me. Restore unto me the joy of thy salvation; and uphold me with thy free spirit. Then will I teach transgressors thy ways; and sinners shall be converted unto thee."

Chapter 3

The Conviction

I was like so many women who did not take the time to count the cost. We get married, broken and not in a place spiritually where we need to be. We marry out of the will and (or) timing of God, and then, we want Him to fix the mess that He warned us not to get into. We borrow the line from the movie *"The Color Purple"*, "I is married now (The Color Purple, Walker, 1982)"! As if those four words are supposed to cause God to change His will or alter His plan for our lives. God tells us not to marry someone and we rebel against the will and word of God, and **when the cost of disobedience begins to require its payment,** we plead for mercy and deliverance and ask God to save the marriage - the marriage that He never intended to take place. We become real religious and start quoting, God's scriptures about the marriage bed being undefiled, as if He doesn't know about our marriage bed. Mine was not the case of me not marrying whom He had chosen for me; my downfall was sin, pure sin, through doubt and unbelief, hurt and rejection.

A couple of weeks after I slept with him, I came under heavy conviction. I went to a R. W. Schambach Revival and repented and asked Jesus to come and live in me, "try me again Lord, try me again", I asked and He did.

I repented of the lust, the bitterness and everything else that was attached to a spirit that I knew nothing about at the time, but later on, I would learn how to fight in the spirit like nobody's business. I returned home and told Michael that we couldn't continue in sin. He agreed and went back to his apartment.

Conviction, is not a word or a feeling that many people readily embrace. But conviction leads to repentance, at least it should, and repentance leads an individual back into the grace and presence of God. Conviction is always going to be from God and a spirit of condemnation is always going to be from the enemy. The enemy will entice you to sin and rebel against God and after you do, he makes you feel too guilty to go to God and ask for forgiveness. Satan wants you to stay in a cycle of shame, guilt and sadness, with feelings of hopelessness and despair.

DREEMM is a ministry founded by my husband and I, and a group of awesome believers, and the DREEMM motto is, "we help families and individuals break cycles". Most people don't even realize that they are in a cycle. They rather feel they are in a tunnel spiraling down out of control.

I had truly repented; truly made up my mind that I was not going to sin and sleep with Michael again. I truly started walking my deliverance out. I felt so good.

The revival that night with R.W. Schambach had been televised live on Trinity Broadcasting Network. I started getting phone calls of people telling me that they had seen me and saw me repent and the whole nine yards. Two weeks later I started having morning sickness. Oh no! The same people that saw me repent, will now see me pregnant. The shame, the guilt, the depression, the despair, they all seemed to have gained up on me at once.

Remember demons travel in groups, but I was too distraught to even recognize demonic spirits. I attended a traditional Baptist church and demons were not part of the curriculum. This battle took such a toll on me that my body begin to turn on itself. I lost

30 pounds in 27 days of my first trimester. I had no strength and no will to live. Because I had entertained several spirits and did not submit to God and resist the devil, the devil and his cohorts were after my destiny, after my gifts, after my assignment, and after my seed.

Mike pleaded with me to fight. He loved me and he wanted this baby so badly. You see, one of the things that I had written in my letter to God, was that I wanted a man/a husband, who had been married before, but had no children. I wanted a father for my girls and I did not want them to have to compete for love or attention. This was Michael's first child. As I lie almost lifeless on the sofa, he knelt down on the floor crying and pleading with me to fight for the child.

LISTEN! Demons do not fight fair. They are not sympathetic. They do not care about you or your children. Their goal is to take out generations at a time if they can, and when you don't know this, you offer them no resistance. My goal in this text is to help you recognize the demonic presences and intended activity in your life.

When you find yourself in an intense spiritual battle, it's not always because of where you are or where you came from; oftentimes, it is where you are going. The enemy knows whose destiny is going to pose the biggest threat to his kingdom, and if he can stop you before you

> *Those demons were trying to steal a destiny that I didn't even know belong to me. They tried to kill a ministry that had not even been conceived in my mind, and they tried to destroy a marriage that was just beginning.*

know who you are and whose you are, he will. After repentance and the struggle to forgive myself, I finally began to pray.

> Psalm 35 (AMP) - Prayer for Rescue from Enemies "Contend, O LORD, with those who contend with me; Fight against those who fight against me. Take hold of shield and buckler (small shield), And stand up for my help. Draw also the spear and javelin to meet those who pursue me. Say to my soul, "I am your salvation." Let those be ashamed and dishonored who seek my life; Let those be turned back [in defeat] and humiliated who plot evil against me. Let them be [blown away] like chaff before the wind [worthless, without substance], With the angel of the LORD driving them on. Let their way be dark and slippery, With the angel of the LORD pursuing and harassing them. For without cause they hid their net for me; Without cause they dug a pit [of destruction] for my life. Let destruction come upon my enemy by surprise; Let the net he hid for me catch him; Into that very destruction let him fall. Then my soul shall rejoice in the LORD; It shall rejoice in His salvation. All my bones will say, "LORD, who is like You, Who rescues the afflicted from him who is too strong for him [to resist alone], And the afflicted and the needy from him who robs him?" Malicious witnesses rise up; They ask me of things that I do not know. They repay me evil for good, To the sorrow of my soul. But as for me, when they were sick, my clothing was sackcloth (mourning garment); I humbled my soul with fasting, And I prayed with my head bowed on my chest. I behaved as if grieving for my friend or my brother; I bowed down in mourning, as one who sorrows for his mother. But in my stumbling they rejoiced and gathered together [against me]; The slanderers whom I did not know

gathered against me; They slandered and reviled me without ceasing. Like godless jesters at a feast, They gnashed at me with their teeth [in malice]. LORD, how long will You look on [without action]? Rescue my life from their destructions, My only life from the young lions. I will give You thanks in the great congregation; I will praise You among a mighty people. Do not let those who are wrongfully my enemies rejoice over me; Nor let those who hate me without cause wink their eye [maliciously]. For they do not speak peace, But they devise deceitful words [half-truths and lies] against those who are quiet in the land. They open their mouths wide against me; They say, "Aha, aha, our eyes have seen it!" You have seen this, O LORD; do not keep silent. O Lord, do not be far from me. Wake Yourself up, and arise to my right And to my cause, my God and my Lord. Judge me, O LORD my God, according to Your righteousness and justice; And do not let them rejoice over me. Do not let them say in their heart, "Aha, that is what we wanted!" Do not let them say, "We have swallowed him up and destroyed him." Let those be ashamed and humiliated together who rejoice at my distress; Let those be clothed with shame and dishonor who magnify themselves over me. Let them shout for joy and rejoice, who favor my vindication and want what is right for me; Let them say continually, "Let the LORD be magnified, who delights and takes pleasure in the prosperity of His servant." And my tongue shall declare Your righteousness (justice), And Your praise all the day long."

Psalm 34:4-7 Amplified Bible (AMP) "I sought the LORD [on the authority of His word], and He answered me, And delivered me from all my fears. They looked to Him and were radiant; Their faces will never blush in shame or confusion. This poor man cried, and the LORD heard him And saved him from all his troubles. The angel of the LORD encamps around those who fear Him [with awe-inspired reverence and worship Him with obedience], **And He rescues [each of] them.**"

Yes, I was the poor man that cried out to God, and He rescued and healed me. I was unable to return to work, but God provided. My husband took good care of the girls and I. As I reflect on that time, my heart is filled with the warmth of those memories. For a while, each time, every other week, he was buying me a new maternity outfit. Although, I was now a stay at home mom, he still wanted me to look just as nice as I did before I got pregnant. So, just a note to the ladies, men will take notice of how you start out with them and treat you accordingly; therefore start out the way that you want to continue and end.

PRAYER FOCUS: Dear Father, thank you for loving me enough to bring me to conviction. Purge me from all evil so that there is no variance within me. Help me to hide your word in my heart and order my steps as well as my conversation.

REMEMBER:

- Conviction is always going to be from God and a spirit of condemnation is always going to be from the enemy.
- REPENT, REPENT, REPENT.
- Forgive yourself.
- The enemy is after your destiny and purpose.
- Demons are not compassionate.
- Demons do not fight fair, they will team up against you.

- When you do not know how to fight in prayer with words from your heart, always pray the scriptures. Give God back His Words.
- The cost of disobedience will always require payment.
- Connect with a deliverance ministry or team that can help you break the cycles.

PRAYER STRATEGY: Psalm 61:1-3 (AMP) "Hear my cry, O God; Listen to my prayer. From the end of the earth I call to You, when my heart is overwhelmed and weak; Lead me to the rock that is higher than I [a rock that is too high to reach without Your help]. For You have been a shelter and a refuge for me, A strong tower against the enemy."

Chapter 4

The Marital Bliss

The damage in my life was done, the blow had been inflicted, the battle had been set with demonic forces in array, and I didn't even know it. Michael and I got married in 1986; this was our year. We purchased our first home, had our daughter, and we purchased a car the same year. We had great friends; we went on our first vacation together. Michael enrolled the girls into bowling and taught them to love the game. He then became their softball coach, and taught them how not to pitch like girls. Life was good.

I left the traditional Baptist church where demons and deliverance were not discussed and went back to a small church called St. James Church of the Triumph, where a 4'-9" General of Generals named Pastor Martha McDaniel Williams taught me about spiritual warfare and modeled how to fight the unseen enemy manifesting through people I knew and loved. I did not know that this equipping would be vital to me as a Minister in the Gospel and Instructor in Deliverance.

I worked at night, so a couple of days during the week I would spend the afternoons with her. I didn't know that I was in a classroom at the time, I thought that I was just helping her. Meanwhile, she was modeling and I was watching; she was coaching and I was listening; she was teaching and I was learning. The longer I stayed in the classroom, the more my spiritual gifts began to activate. I could not only see in the spirit but now I could hear. I was turning into "MaDear" after all, and all fears were dissipating. My running days were behind me.

As the gifts started to activate and my relationship with God became more and more precious, my relationship with my husband became stagnant. He refused to go to church with me and the girls on Sundays. We started out our marriage doing everything together, even going to the grocery store together; but now that we had a second car, he became comfortable with me doing things without him. Initially, I fought him on it, but he was stubborn. I knew I was in a fight, but was unsure as to what type of fight. Was there another woman? Where was the scent of the perfume? Where were the unexplained restaurant receipts? Where were the late night calls? As I pondered on these questions and others like them, I would soon realize that my enemy was not flesh and blood.

A recipe for disaster, we worked opposite shifts. He was off on the weekends and my off days rotated. Things were changing. There was something there, something looming; something working behind the scenes of what was once the "happy family". It was an invitation from my husband's soul to the very spirit that changed my life, the very spirit that I had bound and cast away from me. It was the very spirit (Jezebel) I had resisted so that it had to flee. Yes, that spirit; the manipulation, the anger, the bitterness and the perversion were now manifesting in my husband, but why? Where did it come from?

You see, it would be years later before I would realize the damage that I had caused to his belief system when I seduced him and enticed him to sleep with me. My husband had lost respect for me as it related to my faith. Since I didn't value my faith at the time, neither would he later. Now years later, I would see the fruit of the seeds that I had sown and now I was reaping them.

I would often ask him to accompany the girls and I to church and he would not, unless the kids were in a special program. He would never tell me why, but got extremely annoyed at my asking.

> Galatians 6:7-8 (AMP) "Do not be deceived, God is not mocked [He will not allow Himself to be ridiculed, nor treated with contempt nor allow His precepts to be scornfully set aside]; for whatever a man sows, this and this only is what he will reap. For the one who sows to his flesh [his sinful capacity, his worldliness, his disgraceful impulses] will reap from the flesh ruin and destruction, but the one who sows to the Spirit will from the Spirit reap eternal life."

Wikipedia defines perversion as a type of human behavior that deviates from that which is understood to be orthodox or normal. Although the term perversion can refer to a variety of forms of deviation, it is most often used to describe sexual behaviors that are considered particularly abnormal, repulsive or obsessive. However, for this teaching, we will consider that spiritual perversion is behavior that goes against the Word of God and the Will of God for your life. Behavior that perverts the original intentions of God's plan for you.[1]

1 https://en.wikipedia.org/wiki/Perversion (Wikipedia - the free Encyclopedia)

What was happening? We were having less and less to talk about and Michael was comfortable with that. This would be the start of my understanding the "Little Boy Syndrome". My husband was hurting, and I didn't understand it. He had layers of rejection and many wounds, but at that time I didn't know it. All I knew, was that he was angry at me, angry at God, and angry at the world. All he wanted was food, his couch, television remote, and his computer.

He once scorned me, saying that I was not June Cleaver. I didn't work when we first got married and I did what my mom had modeled before me. I kept myself dressed nicely; my hair was always done. I kept the girls looking lovely. I cooked dinner just about every day (five - six days a week). I kept my home clean. I was the epitome of the virtuous woman, with the exception of, "The heart of her husband trusts in her [with secure confidence] (Proverbs 31:11)".

I soon went back to work and one day (I was working nights then), I stayed up all day. I cooked a Sunday dinner in the middle of the week, then I went out and cut the grass, so he wouldn't have to do anything but come in and relax. I had never cut grass in my life, but I was going to win this battle for my marriage. [Oh, the June Cleaver comment, I cut the grass with a dress on. I have to laugh at myself, when I reflect on those days.] I finished just as he arrived home and I had placed the ladder on the wall right before he pulled into the garage. When he got out of the car and closed the door, the ladder fell onto his car and placed a small dent on the hood. He was furious, so furious, that nothing I did that day was meaningful to him. He even yelled because the grass was cut too short. I went inside, showered and left for work.

I cried all the way to work but with one comforting thought. What I did, I did from my heart and there was nothing the enemy could do about that. My girls were going to have a good dinner that night and the house was clean so no one had any chores to do.

During this battle, you must remember who the battle is against; it is not flesh and blood that you are wrestling with. You have to know that if the enemy is trying really hard to destroy your marriage, then there is great purpose and work for the two of you to do. You just have to be determined that you win, because Jesus has already won.

As Jesus said to Peter, I now say to you, "Satan has asked for you by name and desires to sift you as wheat (Luke 22:31)". Remember, Jesus has prayed for you and the Holy Spirit is present to help you. Moreover, the angels are here to fight on your behalf.

Let us review a few of the spiritual infidelity signs:

- *He/she begins to withdraw physically and emotionally.*
- *Your spouse begins to isolate from you and the family.*
- *Your spouse begins the "blame game" or fault-finding.*
- *Your spouse becomes easily irritated with you and the children.*
- *Finances become an issue, when they shouldn't be.*

PRAYER FOCUS - Father, I thank you for the finished work of the cross. Because of it, I am no longer condemned by my past. I humbly accept your forgiveness for my impatience and wholeheartedly accept your grace. Help me to extend the same measure of grace to my spouse that you extended to me.

REMEMBER:

- As long as your identity is hidden from you, you are not a threat to the enemy.
- The enemy will not attack your marriage unless you become a threat to his kingdom.
- Your spouse is not your enemy.
- Spend quality time together to reduce the chances of the enemy coming in.
- Pray together, but if the enemy is present, and your spouse doesn't want to pray, YOU MUST PRAY.
- Little by little satan wants to sift your marriage, until there is no marriage and the covenant is destroyed.
- You have the victory through Christ Jesus.

PRAYER STRATEGY - Matthew 6:20-21 (KJV) "But lay up for yourselves treasures in heaven, where neither moth nor rust doth corrupt, and where thieves do not break through nor steal: For where your treasure is, there will your heart be also."

Chapter 5

The Awakening

I began to notice that the stronger I became spiritually, the clearer my identity became. The more I learned about my gifts, the stronger their activation became. As I began to increase in wisdom, knowledge and understanding, so did the problems in my marriage. A team of demons began to advance to the point that they lost their cover. I recognized them and their activity. They not only were after my marriage but they had come for my girls also.

DON'T COME FOR MY GIRLS!!!

My youngest daughter would see a tall figure standing at the top of the steps in our home. This absolutely terrified her and she said her stuffed animal, Alf, would wake up and try to bite her at night. We had to dispose of the toy.

One Sunday night (after I started back working on Sunday's), I got off work around 11:30 pm. I was in the house maybe ten minutes when I heard my middle daughter screaming. She was in the middle of her bed trembling and screaming. A demon had manifested in her room. My husband came on the scene with a weapon, but that weapon would be no match for this spirit.

My mom says that as a child I was a bully, but now I had to learn to be a bully in the spirit. As a child there were four other girls that backed me up when I got into fights, but now I had the hosts of heaven, the angels of the Lord, all fighting for me and with me.

When it comes to warfare, we can't just sit back and say, "Please Mr. Demon. leave my family alone." Rather, we have to become skilled at using the weapons provided for us and utilize those weapons with all of the power and authority given us through and by the Word of the Lord.

> 2 Corinthians 10:3-6 (ESV) " For though we walk in the flesh, we are not waging war according to the flesh. For the weapons of our warfare are not of the flesh but have divine power to destroy strongholds. We destroy arguments and every lofty opinion raised against the knowledge of God, and take every thought captive to obey Christ, being ready to punish every disobedience, when your obedience is complete."

> Luke 10:18-20 (AMP) "He said to them, "I watched Satan fall from heaven like [a flash of] lightning. Listen carefully: I have given you authority [that you now possess] to tread on serpents and scorpions, and [the ability to exercise authority] over all the power of the enemy (Satan); and nothing will [in any way] harm you. Nevertheless do not rejoice at this, that the spirits are subject to you, but rejoice that your names are recorded in heaven."

I fought and fought through prayer, worship, fasting and I warred in the spirit like a true ninja. Learning to use the Sword of the Spirit is vital during warfare. I prayed so fervently in my home that once a young lady visited and asked me why there were so many ladders in my living room. She begin to look at every wall and then asked me what were the angels doing, going back and forth on the ladders. This was amazing insight into the spiritual realm revealing what prayer was accomplishing in my home.

God would send me different life jackets to hold on to. Deliverance was not a part of my understanding or arsenal at that time, at least not like it is today. I worked hard.

Despite my spouse's behavior, I tried to care for my girls in such a way that they wouldn't feel the blunt of the battles going on in our home. During those years, I survived off of 2 to 4 hours of sleep a day; unless it was my off days. The girls were in 3 different schools. I still worked ten to twelve hours a day (mandatory). I continued as the "room mom" for my youngest daughter at her elementary school and my oldest daughter wanted to start a gospel choir at the high school where they needed a parent to head it. Because of my background in music I accepted the role. Was I a glutton for punishment or was this a survival technique?

I believe it was survival or a form of escapism. I stayed busy so I would not have to deal with things in my natural reality. This was not the right way to handle things. Please, listen to me, this is called an escape tactic. Unless you are running into the presence of God, this can be one of your biggest down falls. I became mentally and spiritually

Escapism, From Wikipedia, the free encyclopedia, is the avoidance of unpleasant, boring, arduous, scary, or banal aspects of daily life. It can also be used as a term to define the actions people take to help relieve persisting feelings of depression or general sadness.[2]

2 https://en.wikipedia.org/wiki/Escapism (Wikipedia - the free Encyclopedia)

drained, because I was giving out faster than I could replenish or replace. Eventually, I started to make decisions and choices that would give the enemy increased access to my marriage and my girls.

Know this, if the enemy can keep you in a state of depression or sadness, he knows that you will be too distracted to fight him. After pulling myself together, I began to strap on my weapons as if I were Rambo. This territory was somewhat unfamiliar to me and my prayer level had to intensify. The enemy had turned up the heat. There was trouble in my home. The relationships with the women and friends I knew at church had begun to dissolve; and my supervisor was an atheist/witch who made it her personal vendetta to try to eliminate my job. This is the representation of the manifestation of the spirit of python. When you are attacked in more than one area of your life, you can be sure that python is present to squeeze the very breath/life out of you.

Valentine's Day weekend was coming up, and I decided I was going to walk away from everything that was stressing me and plan a romantic weekend with my husband. I had placed a beautiful red dress on hold at one of the major department stores. I made reservations for dinner, and went to get my hair done. My hair was pretty, long, thick, and healthy, at least I thought so. As my stylist was putting my relaxer in, she told me to run to the shampoo bowl. As I sat there tears began to run down her face. I asked her what was wrong and she said, my hair had just fallen out. I didn't know what to think. Another patron whom I didn't know, was there and she came and knelt down beside me and began to pray. My stylist and I went to the same doctor so she called the doctor and told her what happened and they directed me to a dermatology specialist immediately. They placed a plastic cap on my head. I could see hair through the cap, so I didn't understand what was going on. They did not want me to drive therefore asked if I wanted them to call my husband. I immediately said no, because if I was truly bald, I didn't want him to see me, so I opted for them to call my parents. I didn't take the cap off and look into the mirror until I arrived at the doctor's office. When I did, I immediately began to scream. The hair I saw through the cap was only at the top of my head. I still had the length, therefore through the cap, I didn't realize that the only hair left on my head was that at the very top. From one side to the other it looked as if someone had taken a razor and shaved off all of my hair.

I know some of you may be thinking, did she really get that upset over her hair. The answer is emphatically, yes! I keep my hair cut now because it is my choice and my desire. At that time, going to the salon one way and leaving a totally different way, was traumatic for me.

The enemy was after my identity, inwardly and outwardly. He was after my husband's identity. He was after my daughter's identity. Darts were coming from multiple directions, and I wasn't skilled enough in the spirit to quench them all or dodge them. After getting myself together, I remember reading in 1 Samuel: "And the women answered one another as they played, and said, Saul hath slain his thousands, and David his ten thousand".

Now, I needed to be taught the art of war by the Holy Spirit, so that I could pursue that which was pursuing me; so that I could discomfort that which was discomforting me and slay thousands at a time.

The Manifestation of Python

The perimeter of the attack began to widen. Not only was I being attacked at home but at work. When attacks are coming from multiple areas at one time, you know that *the spirit of python* is manifesting. Its job is to weary you in every area, until you have no more strength or desire to fight.

You've read in scripture (Romans 8:28), "And we know that all things work together for good to them that love God, to them *who are the called according to his purpose."* I was about to experience this scripture.

My supervisor at the time, a professed atheist, was trying to prove that I could not do my job due to an injury and she did not want to create another job for me, per union contract. So, for months I clocked in for work and sat in the women's locker room 6 to 10 hours a day and studied my Bible and other books. I know $50,000 may not be a lot of money to some people, but eighteen years ago it was a lot to me. I was being paid to train for the Kingdom of God, being paid to become equipped for God's purposes, and being paid to become a threat to the kingdom of darkness. All things really do work out for the good of those who truly love the Lord.

I studied and I studied; I prayed and I prayed; I grew and I grew. I went back to school to get my Masters, and continued to grow. This growth also included more and more attacks from the enemy. They were no longer subtle, but God! God was there, talking to me, telling me where to go and what to do. He was showing me where the next attacks were coming from, equipping me, strengthening me, and providing grace for the journey.

Wives, listen to me. You may be feeling tired and overwhelmed, but don't give up. Don't stop unless you are ordered to do so by the Holy Spirit. God will prepare a time and place for you to come into His Presence and learn from Him. The following are some things that you can expect to happen:

• God will purge you first. Some things are allowed to happen because the soil of your heart is being tilled and ready for planting. The Holy Spirit will begin to prune you because in the process of life and the attack of your marriage, you may have some bitter weeds or maybe you attracted some type of garden bugs (**anger, lust, resentment, perversion, and/or addiction**) that are trying to eat up your flower (that which helps you bloom beautifully). The healing of your marriage and the restoration of your family is going to start with you. God has to have a way into your marriage and if your husband has been seduced by the enemy, you are going to have to be the door in which the Father enters into the situation.

• You can expect to feel alone at times, as if you are in the middle of the ocean with the water heaped up around you, but know that God is lifting a standard against the enemy. God will not allow the waters to overtake you. During times like these, increase your worship and build your arsenal. Ask the Holy Spirit to prescribe specific scriptures for you, as a medical doctor would prescribe medication. Make sure you take/read and meditate on those scriptures several times a day. *The Word Will do the Work!*

• Now that the enemy knows that you are aware of him and that you are fighting to win, he may come with multiple attacks at one time. This is when you know that the ***spirit of python*** has been deployed against you.

• ***Have no fear,*** for, "The word of God is quick, and powerful, and sharper than any ***two-edged-sword***, piercing even to the dividing asunder of soul and spirit, and of the joints and marrow, and is a discerner of the thoughts and intents of the heart (Hebrews 4:12)." Take this sword and cut into pieces that which is trying to squeeze the life out of you. In the natural a python (snake) wraps around you and each time you take a breath, he tightens his grip until all of your organs are squeezed with no oxygen circulating. He has to get you to a place where there is no more fight in you so that he can devour you without any resistance on your part. It is the same way with the python spirit, the enemy wants to weaken you and get you to the place where you have no fight in you, so that you will offer no resistance.

• Remember James 4:7, "Submit yourselves therefore to God. Resist the devil, and he will flee from you". Use the sword of the spirit; don't let the enemy immobilize you; you immobilize him; with the Word and your worship. Worship will confuse the enemy every time. Paul and Silas worshipped after they had been beaten and incarcerated and their bands and those of the other prisoners were broken off. Paul was beaten and incarcerated and he began to worship by writing the letters and the epistles that we read today. The Apostle John worshipped with his testimony and witness of his brother, so that even when he was boiled in oil, he survived. I worshipped with the fruit of my hand as I started my own catering company. Whether I cooked a meal for 5 or 1500, I did it with prayer and worship. When we had chicken my partner, Sis. Yvonne, would pray over every piece of chicken while she was cleaning them. We learned how to worship as we cooked and God was honored. Moreover, we had a good name as a catering business.

Proverbs 22:1-3 (KJV) "A good name is rather to be chosen than great riches, and loving favour rather than silver and gold."

• You may find yourself in transition, or at least developing a taste for other foods (other ministries). Be CAREFUL and be PRAYERFUL. If your pastor is not skilled or open to deliverance ministry, **ask the Holy Spirit to direct you to someone or some ministry that is skilled in deliverance.** Going to a conference is NOT ENOUGH. You don't need a feel-good thrill. You need someone who is skilled in warfare and discernment and who will be able to walk with you.

• **Disappointments will come, but don't allow weariness to overtake you.** You will have good days in your marriage and think that everything is going to be okay, and then the enemy will strike a blow. It is okay, because everything will be okay. The enemy is not going to sit still and allow you to throw one punch after the other without retaliating.

• *Remember this:* Each day BIND-up the *spirit of backlash and retaliation*. When the enemy strikes back, you just have to set your footing and begin to shoot with your automatic weapons: *your tongue, your hands, and your praise.* This is why it is so important to develop a scripture base as your arsenal. Don't believe the lies of the enemy. The spirit of wicker, that "ole serpent" knows just how much scriptural truth to mix with his lies.

• Do not get caught-up in the lies of the enemy; rather confess and believe the Word of God. Keep the belt of truth on at all times and learn how to quench fiery darts because they will come.

• As my daughter would say, "with everything you do wrap it all up in love". Love will motivate you and **Love** will give you the power and strength that you need to overcome the enemy and snatch your husband and family from the grip of the enemy. Love is like the *jaws of life* freeing your loved ones from bent irons and metal from a twisted and bent up vehicle. Whether that vehicle is lust, adultery, fornication, perversion, lies, strife, bitterness or hatred; your consistent love in this battle will free them. For God so love the world that He gave. During this battle, you will have a clearer understanding of what *"so loved"* really means. You will learn how to truly give: Give of yourself and your right to be right; your feelings; your time; your tears; and sometimes your voice.

> Matthew 18:18 (AMP) "I assure you and most solemnly say to you, whatever you bind [forbid, declare to be improper and unlawful] on earth shall have [already] been bound in heaven, and whatever you loose [permit, declare lawful] on earth shall have [already] been loosed in heaven."

• **Worship will have to become a lifestyle for you.** You cannot get comfortable in your victories. After you have defeated the enemy, he will regroup and study you and your family waiting for the next opportunity to attack. After a victory, if possible, educate and provided knowledge to your family. Teach them to ask the Holy Spirit for wisdom. The more their eyes are opened the more sweat-less your victories will become. Remember when God is with you as your Rock, one of you will chase a thousand and two will put two thousand to flight.

Deuteronomy 32 informs us that when Israel walked upright before God their victory against their enemy was so secure that the only way their enemies could defeat them was when they (Israel) rebelled against God. With the power of the Holy Spirit and the Word of God, you have been equipped to fight and win the battle against the enemy for you and your family. As their eyes are opened, rebellion will have no place in their hearts and therefore, your victory too will be secure in God, for He is your Rock.

Following are additional weapons that I learned to use during this season of my life. I would ask God to fight against my enemies utilizing these weapons.

1) Weapon: The Arrow of the Lord

II Kings 13:17 "And he said, "Open the east window"; and he opened it. Then Elisha said, "Shoot"; and he shot. And he said, **"The arrow of the Lord's deliverance** and the **arrow** of deliverance from Syria; for you must strike the Syrians at Aphek till you have destroyed them."

2) Weapon: The Consuming Fire

Deuteronomy 4:23-24 (AMP) "So be on your guard and watch yourselves, so that you do not forget the covenant of the LORD your God which He has made with you ... **For the LORD your God is a consuming fire;** He is a jealous (impassioned) God [demanding what is rightfully and uniquely His]."

3) Weapon: The Net of the Lord

Hosea 7:10, 12 (AMP) "Though the pride of Israel testifies against him, Yet they do not return [in repentance] to the LORD their God, Nor seek nor search for nor desire Him [as essential] in spite of all this ... When they go, **I will spread My net over them;** I will bring them down like birds of the heavens [into Assyrian captivity]. I will chastise them in accordance with the proclamation (prophecy) to their congregation."

4) Weapon: Thunder

1 Samuel 7:9-14 (NKJV) "And Samuel took a suckling lamb and offered it as a whole burnt offering to the LORD. Then Samuel cried out to the LORD for Israel, and the LORD answered him. Now as Samuel was offering up the burnt offering, the Philistines drew near to battle against Israel. **But the LORD thundered with a loud thunder** upon the Philistines that day, and so confused them that they were overcome before Israel. And the men of Israel went out of Mizpah and pursued the Philistines, and drove them back as far as below Beth Car. Then Samuel took a stone and set it up between Mizpah and Shen, and called its name Ebenezer, [a] saying, 'Thus far the LORD has helped us.' So the Philistines were subdued, and they did not come anymore into the territory of Israel. And the hand of the LORD was against the Philistines all the days of Samuel. **Then the cities which the Philistines had taken from Israel were restored to Israel, from Ekron to Gath; and Israel recovered its territory from the hands of the Philistines. Also there was peace between Israel and the Amorites."**

5) Weapon: Stumbling-Block

Jeremiah 6:21 (NKJV) "Therefore thus says the LORD: "Behold, **I will lay stumbling blocks** before this people, And the fathers and the sons together shall fall on them. The neighbor and his friend shall perish."

PRAYER FOCUS: James 2:18-22 (ESV) "But someone will say, 'You have faith and I have works.' Show me your faith apart from your works, and I will show you my faith by my works. You believe that God is one; you do well. Even the demons believe — and shudder! Do you want to be shown, you foolish person, that faith apart from works is useless? Was not Abraham our father justified by works when he offered up his son Isaac on the altar? You see that faith was active along with his works, and faith was completed by his works."

Dearest Father,
Increase my faith and teach me how to fight and how to stand, and to know when each is needed and at what time. Help me to separate my anger against the enemy from my love for my husband.

REMEMBER:
- Worship must become a lifestyle for you.
- The weapons of your warfare are not carnal but mighty through God to the pulling down of strongholds.
- Know your weapons; build your arsenal.
- Rise up early in the morning and command your day: make your decrees and declarations.
- Do not fear, but be strong and courageous.
- Seek Godly counsel and connect with someone who not only has the heart of God but your heart also. Don't be so quick to share what is happening with just anyone. Ask God to send you someone who is skilled enough to assist and teach you.

PRAYER STRATEGY:

Dearest Father,
Permit me to dwell in Your shelter and to abide under Your Shadow. Instruct me in the way that I should go. Help me to recognize the enemy when he is yet a distance away. I believe even as I decree that 1,000 may fall at my side and 10,000 at my right hand but nothing

will not come near my dwelling place, my marriage, or my family. I will continue to decree and release Psalms 1 over my husband. Blessed is Michael who walks not in the counsel of the wicked, nor does Michael stands in the way of sinners, nor does Michael sit in the seat of scoffers; but Michael's delight is in the law of the LORD, and in God's law does Michael meditates day and night. Michael is like a tree planted by streams of water that yields its fruit in its season, and its leaf does not wither. All that Michael does, for the Kingdom of God prospers.

Chapter 6

The Battle

As stated in the Introduction, I repeat now, My hope and my prayer are that as you read the pages of this book, you will be able to recognize the enemy and utilize the tools and strategies I had to learn in battle, so that your fight will not be extended and tedious.

It may only take you a day or so to read this book, but in no way was this book written in a day or two. The information took years to obtain, because the battle went on for years. God allowed it and gave me the strength and grace to endure it; not that I alone could have the victory, but that in these last days, the attack of the enemy would be cut short so that you can go ahead and be about your Father's business rather than fighting a long, drawn out battle. Praise be to God! Jesus had already won the victory for me, and He has won it for you. Stand strong and posture yourself before the Almighty God and He will see you through the battle that is before you.

As the years passed Michael and I had a lot of good days and a lot of unspoken fights. You know, the kind where everything seems normal to everyone else but you know there is still something looming around seeking for an opportunity and waiting to ambush you. This was one of the most challenging times for me. I continued to increase in knowledge, skill, and strength. I was learning more and more about who my God was and who I was in Him. I was going from one degree of glory to the next because of wisdom and understanding. These will be two of the most momentous weapons you will need as you obtain victory, **wisdom** and **understanding.**

> 2 Corinthians 3:17-18 (AMP) "Now the Lord is the Spirit, and where the Spirit of the Lord is, there is liberty [emancipation from bondage, true freedom]. And we all, with unveiled face, continually seeing as in a mirror the glory of the Lord, are progressively being transformed into His image from [one degree of] glory to [even more] glory, which comes from the Lord, [who is] the Spirit."

During this time, I was becoming more aware of the fact, that my husband was having an identity crisis and was not able to comprehend the spiritual attacks or the devices the enemy was using to come against us. I had to be careful and hold my tongue. In other words, I had to watch my words so that the enemy wouldn't get any help from me. I had to remember that I was not wrestling against flesh and blood. During this part of your battle, wanting God to be glorified has to be more important to you than being right or winning an argument with your spouse.

What gave me strength was the realization and understanding that the enemy was after my husband's soul. He wanted my husband separated from God. He was trying to put him to sleep at a time when he wasn't even fully awake. I realized then, that my husband was a sleeping giant; one that the enemy did not want to wake up; one that the enemy was afraid of. You see, that is how the enemy works, he tries to stop you before you realize that you have the authority to stop him. He understands that the anointing flows; therefore he sets traps for you and your children so that no one is left to fight him. This strategy he borrowed from God our Father. Remember, satan is a thief; he steals strategies and war tactics that belong to God. He makes a lot of noise trying to intimidate us and cause us to fear. He saw that it worked when God gave this same strategy to Joshua and later Saul. Be wise; know that with satan, it's just noise. Try shouting a loud "NO" back to him. Tell him that his tricks and tactics are unlawful in the heavens; therefore, they are unlawful in your marriage here on earth.

> Joshua 6:20-21 (AMP) "So the people shouted [the battle cry], and the priests blew the trumpets. When the people heard the sound of the trumpet, they raised a great shout and the wall [of Jericho] fell down, so that the sons of Israel went up into the city, every man straight ahead [climbing over the rubble], and they overthrew the city. Then they utterly destroyed everything that was in the city, both man and woman, young and old, and ox and sheep and donkey, with the edge of the sword."

> 1 Samuel 15:2-3 (KJV) "Thus saith the LORD of hosts, I remember that which Amalek did to Israel, how he laid wait for him in the way, when he came up from Egypt. Now go and smite Amalek, and utterly destroy all that they have, and spare them not; but slay both man and woman, infant and suckling, ox and sheep, camel and ass."

You too may be married to a sleeping giant, if so, keep praying. YOU WIN!!! By this time, I had accepted God's plan for my life as it dealt with deliverance. I realized that there were things all along the various paths and journeys that life had taken me on, which had and were preparing me for this time.

The light began to peak through at the end of the tunnel. My church at the time was preparing for the yearly convocation. It was going to be held in Lexington, Kentucky. This is where my husband was born. Although I was battling for his soul, my emotions had begun to shut down, almost in a self-preservation holding pattern. Similarly, like an airplane when it is waiting for a place to land, I knew I needed this conference, and I felt that I needed some time away from Michael. BUT GOD! God had another plan. Our first grandchild had arrived and I wanted to go to Lexington ahead of time to check out the hotel where I would stay for convocation. I was a very overly protective grandmother, and I was a little particular about the hotel that I would be bringing this newborn into. As I shared my plans with my husband, letting him know I was going down to look at the hotel and choose another one if I had to, he blurted out, "I'll go with you".

At first, I couldn't believe what I heard. Then I had a little talk with Jesus and told Him that my husband could not go with me. I told Him, that this was my time with Him; my time to be refreshed; my time to gather strength. After I told God what time it was, He simply said, **"That is where he was born and it is where he will be re-born.** That shut my mouth and I, like Mary the mother of Jesus, just began to ponder some things in my heart.

PRAYER FOCUS: 1 Peter 5:6-11 (AMP) "Therefore humble yourselves under the mighty hand of God [set aside self-righteous pride], so that He may exalt you [to a place of honor in His service] at the appropriate time, casting all your cares [all your anxieties, all your worries, and all your concerns, once and for all] on Him, for He cares about you [with deepest affection, and watches over you very carefully]. Be sober [well balanced and self-disciplined], be alert and cautious at all times. That enemy of yours, the devil, prowls around like a roaring lion [fiercely hungry], seeking someone to devour. But resist him, be firm in your faith [against his attack—rooted, established, immovable], knowing that the same experiences of suffering are being experienced by your brothers and sisters throughout the world. [You do not suffer alone.] After you have suffered for a little while, the God of all grace [who imparts His blessing and favor], who called you to His own eternal glory in Christ, will Himself complete, confirm, strengthen, and establish you [making you what you ought to be]. To Him be dominion (power, authority, sovereignty) forever and ever. Amen."

REMEMBER:
- Jesus has already won and defeated the enemy.
- Knowledge is power and patience is a necessity.
- Two most important weapons will be wisdom and understanding during this season.
- Time may pass by and it may look as if the enemy has given up, but actually, he is only regrouping and coming back with back-up and a different strategy. You too must strategize for each battle.
- Only strike a blow to the enemy, as the Holy Spirit directs you. You must become a sharp shooter in the spirit to become effective.

PRAYER STRATEGY:
Dear God,
Please help me to lean not unto my own understanding, but rather to trust, lean on, and rely upon you. I know that you have plans for me; plans to prosper me in my marriage and plans for my marriage to be a great representation of your covenant in the earth. Forgive me for being impatient and help me to be steadfast and unmovable despite the storms, knowing that you are in control. Amen.

Chapter 7

The Victory

Submitting to the Will and Plan of God, my husband accompanied me to Lexington to check out the hotel; and yes, we did have to look for a different hotel other than the one where the conference was going to be held. My husband still knew the city pretty well and therefore his presence would be a great asset.

The thought that things were about to change became very intriguing to me and yet I was apprehensive and excited. What would this change look like? Would it be instant? Would it be a process; and if so, how long?

The girls and I went to Lexington ahead of Michael. He had to work and wouldn't be able to come down until that Saturday morning. Saturday, actually from my point of view, was going to be excellent. You see, I had helped God figure out, how this was supposed to go. At least, so I thought! Since I believed he was resistant to women in leadership, his attendance to the Saturday sessions would have been great. There would be powerful anointed men teaching at all three sessions. I was really getting excited now!

Unexpectedly, my husband called saying he was very ill. He didn't know what happened. He had arrived at work and became very dizzy and lightheaded. He wasn't sure if he was going to be able to make it back home from work. He was working downtown Cincinnati, so I heard in the spirit realm, "tell him to cross the bridge" (into Kentucky). I told him what I heard. The Holy Spirit, showed me how the enemy had tightened up its grip on him and was trying to prevent him from reaching his appointed time, his destination, his point of Glory in God. I told Michael, that I was immediately going into prayer and all I needed was for him to cross the river, and the headache and the dizziness would be gone. I didn't know as much then as I do now, but I did know that demons were territorial and assigned to regions. I knew that he had to get out of Cincinnati.

He agreed and therefore I expected to see him by the time the morning session was over and the afternoon session began. My heart dropped when he called and said that his head was hurting so badly that he just couldn't drive the "90 minutes" to Lexington. I became angry and hurt. I had allowed myself to come out of the emotional holding pattern and it looked like the change I had been praying and doing spiritual warfare for was not going to happen. However, I pulled myself together and went into the worship service. As I began to forget about myself and concentrate on God, He showed me a scene from a book that I had been teaching from. The book was *This Present Darkness* by Frank Peretti. There was a scene where the enemy was preparing to attack in one city but God had the angels gathering saints in the surrounding cities to pray. I immediately received the revelation from the vision and grabbed my daughters' hands and told them to battle for their dad. They might have been young, but they prayed that day. We prayed and worshipped until we felt breakthrough.

I called Michael, after the services. I told him that our future son-n-law was coming down to Lexington to propose to our oldest daughter on her birthday, which was the next day. I told him to ride along with him; and he did.

We had warred with the opposing angels and in conjunction with the Will of God, now I was about to see what VICTORY LOOKED LIKE! I was at the hotel getting ready for the final session. I happened to go from my room to my daughters' room. As I did, I saw this man walking down the hall, and thought, "that's a good-looking man". Then, I did a double take and realized that it was my husband. He looked different! He looked brighter! His countenance had changed! His stride was with confidence and determination. I thought to myself, "My, my, my, so this is what victory looks like." The angels of the Lord had fought and won, snatching my husband from the grips of the enemy.

I was happy that Michael was there, but then I thought, "Oh, there is a female pastor closing out the conference." Remember, I told you earlier that I thought I had helped God orchestrate this thing. Normally, when he had visited the church with me, he would always sit in the back, therefore I expected the same now, not realizing how much of a transformation God had already done. So I asked him where did he want to sit and he said it did not matter. So, we went to sit in the middle of the room; only he didn't sit. He stood up and participated in worship. A few minutes later, my pastor came and embraced him and asked him if he would go up front with her. He agreed and as the guest pastor began to release the Word of the Lord, she spoke some things that led her right to him. She asked if he wanted to be free and he said yes. The next thing I knew, he was screaming and jumping at least 2-3 feet up in the air!

As sure as God is Faithful, my husband ran into Power; he ran into Jesus and accepted Him as his Lord and Savior. Jezebel was defeated and my husband experienced the Anointing that destroys the yokes of bondage!

PRAYER FOCUS: Matthew 6:9-13 (KJV) "After this manner therefore pray ye: Our Father which art in heaven, Hallowed be thy name. Thy kingdom come, Thy will be done in earth, as it is in heaven. Give us this day our daily bread. And forgive us our debts, as we forgive our debtors. And lead us not into temptation, but deliver us from evil: For thine is the kingdom, and the power, and the glory, forever. Amen."

REMEMBER:

- The enemy may be strategic, but God created strategy.
- Ask the Holy Spirit to identify the enemy.
- Your circumstances don't change God; God changes your circumstances.
- Don't become weary in well doing (Galatians 6:9).
- Sometimes, the battle is not simply about you; others are waiting on your victory; your testimony.
- When your emotions begin to interfere with your spirit and the plan of God, go into an emotional holding pattern, wait until you have been cleared to land.
- Ask God to develop your hearing so that you can always hear Him; for His ways are not yours ... He has a plan.
- Demons are territorial and assigned to regions.
- There is power in unity and agreement; ask God to send you someone that will help you. It may surprise you, who He sends.

PRAYER STRATEGY:

Dear God,
You have been my dwelling place. You are from everlasting to everlasting. Your thoughts are higher than our thoughts and therefore we trust you to lead and guide us. You and only you know your plans towards us.

Epilogue

It is one thing when your husband's heart has been lured away from you by another woman, but what happens when it's something you can't see, touch or feel? What happens when you can't smell their perfume and when there's no lipstick on his collar and no unknown text or phone number?

This is when you will need to be *The Wife, The Warrior.* You will begin to realize that you need, *Help! Jezebel Has Seduced Your Husband.* In the interm, equip yourself by knowing who Jezebel is and becoming familiar with her seductive strategies. Although you may experience very "real" battles, when you apply the Biblical strategies in this book, victory is inevitable!

GLOSSARY

Accuser Of The Brethren - *(Revelation 12:9-11, KJV)* - Accusation is one of the weapons that satan tries to use against us. He uses our mind as his battlefield and releases thoughts and suggestive images against others, to us, and often times about us also. His plan is to target our consciences so that our heart will become bitter towards others and towards God. He wants us to succumb to unforgiveness and bitterness and to be filled with so much guilt that depression sets in and immobilizes us. Remember Job.

Anger - *(1 Timothy 2:8, AMP)* - Anger can be defined as a strong feeling of displeasure and usually of antagonism. The spirit of anger is usually rooted out of a spirit of fear and thereby becomes united with blinding and blocking spirits. These prevent you from seeing or recognizing truth and reality. Your vision becomes blinded by the false reality that the enemy has built up in your mind.

Bitterness - *(Ephesians 4:27-31, AMP)* - A feeling of deep anger and resentment. It is an emotion which encompasses both anger and hate. Bitterness is the unchallenged resulted of anger and rejection lodged in one's soul.

Blinding Spirit - *(Genesis 19:10-11 AMP)* - The act of concealing or masking the truth. These spirits often work with a spirit called "wicker" (wicker meaning to twist). In the natural wicker is a slender, flexible (easily swayed) twig that is used to bend into the shape of your choice. In the spirit it is the bending of an unsteady thought (doubt) that causes truth to be twisted.

Blocking Spirits - *(Genesis 18:21-25, MSG) (Numbers 22:21-25, MSG)* - We must understand that satan is a counterfeiter. He attempts to emulate everything, every action that is revealed through the word, plan, and purpose of God. In the light of this scripture to block means to hinder, obstruct, delay or detain. However, we must keep in mind that God will also block our blessings when we fall into sin.

Caging Spirits - *(Revelation 18:1-3, KJV)* - These spirits want you to be imprisoned as they were before their release. Caging is the act of placing or trapping something in a cage. Caging Spirits are a group of unclean spirits whose attacks include bombarding you until you have no reflection of any of God's characteristics. The weapons and tools that the enemy uses for spiritual caging are designed to trap, hinder, stop, lockdown, and confine your purpose and destiny.

Familiar Spirits - *(Leviticus 19:30-32)* Familiar has its roots from a Latin word "familiaris" which means "household servant." Biblical History informs us that witches would utilize these spirits to help them with their magic. These spirits can only gain access to you, if there is an open door (such as: witchcraft, divination, fear, meditation, drugs, perversion/sexual and addiction, etc.).

Generational Curses And Cycles - *(Exodus 34:7, KJV)* - Generational curses have to do with lifestyles patterns and choices. As it is in the medical field so it is in the spiritual realm. Just as you are genetically prone to have certain diseases and ailments that were passed down to you from your parents or grandparents through your bloodline; so are you prone to have demonic manifestation, that cycles through your family of origin by way of sin. Both call for a turning away from - a repentance. If your family members are prone to have hypertension, then you need to turn away from the foods and lifestyle choices that will ensure that you will have high blood pressure. If there are repetitious cycles of addiction, then you need to avoid atmospheres and relationships that will lure you into the world of addiction/perversion.

Mind-Controlling Spirits (Witchcraft) - *(2 Thessalonians 2:1-3, KJV and Philippians 4:7, KJV)* Mind control, also known as brain washing, is aimed at destroying a person's basic convictions and attitudes and replacing them with an alternative set of beliefs. It is a common practice in witchcraft. The Bible urges us to not only gird up the loins of our mind but to look at how Christ thought and acted and let that be our guide and pattern.

Spirit Of Deception - *(Jeremiah 3:9-11)* - Deception can be defined as the act of causing someone to accept as true or valid what is false or invalid. The spirit of deception, as with most demons, works within your thought patterns and process trying to connect with untruths that have been lodged in your soul.

Spirit Of Perversion - *(Leviticus 18:22-24 & 1 Corinthians 6:9-10)* Perversion can be defined as the alteration of something from its original course, meaning, or state to a distortion or corruption of what was first intended. The above-mentioned scripture clearly illustrates that perversion leads to defilement. Anything that alters the original intent of the word, purpose, and plan of God for your life is perverted.

Spirit Of Pride - *(1 Peter 5:5-7, AMP)* Pride can be defined as a feeling or deep pleasure or satisfaction derived from one's own achievements, the achievements of those with whom one is closely associated, or from qualities or possessions that are widely admired.

Although we are to have confidence in ourselves, we can become boastful, when we begin to think more highly of ourselves then we should.

Spirit Of Python - *(Genesis 3:1-13 and Acts 16:16)* Python is also known as a spirit of divination. It operates in the spirit just as it operates in the natural. It squeezes the life out of its victims, suffocating them. The signs of this spirit are indicated by and through depression, oppression, heaviness, fatigue, confusion and discouragement. You begin to doubt everything and everybody including God. You begin to feel depleted and lifeless and feel that you will never be able to break its hold on you.

Spirit Of Rejection - *(Numbers 14:11 and 1 Samuel 8:7)* Rejection can be defined as to refuse to accept, consider, submit to, take for some purpose, or use; to refuse or separate from a person or thing. In deliverance, rejection is the number 1 spirit that we encounter. We were created to belong, and when there is a certain group or person pushing us away, the emotional feeling of rejection manifests. If this is not dealt with, a spirit will attach itself to the emotion.

Spirit Spouses (Incubus & Succubus) - *(Genesis 6:1-3)* - Incubus is an evil spirit that lies on persons in their sleep; especially : one that has sexual intercourse with women while they are sleeping. Succubus is a demon assuming female form to have sexual intercourse with men in their sleep.

Strife - *(Proverbs 20:3)* Strife can be defined as a bitter quarrel or struggle or conflict and discord with another. In deliverance, strife is a frequent weapon used by the enemy in marriages.

www.ingramcontent.com/pod-product-compliance
Lightning Source LLC
LaVergne TN
LVHW051706080426
835511LV00017B/2768